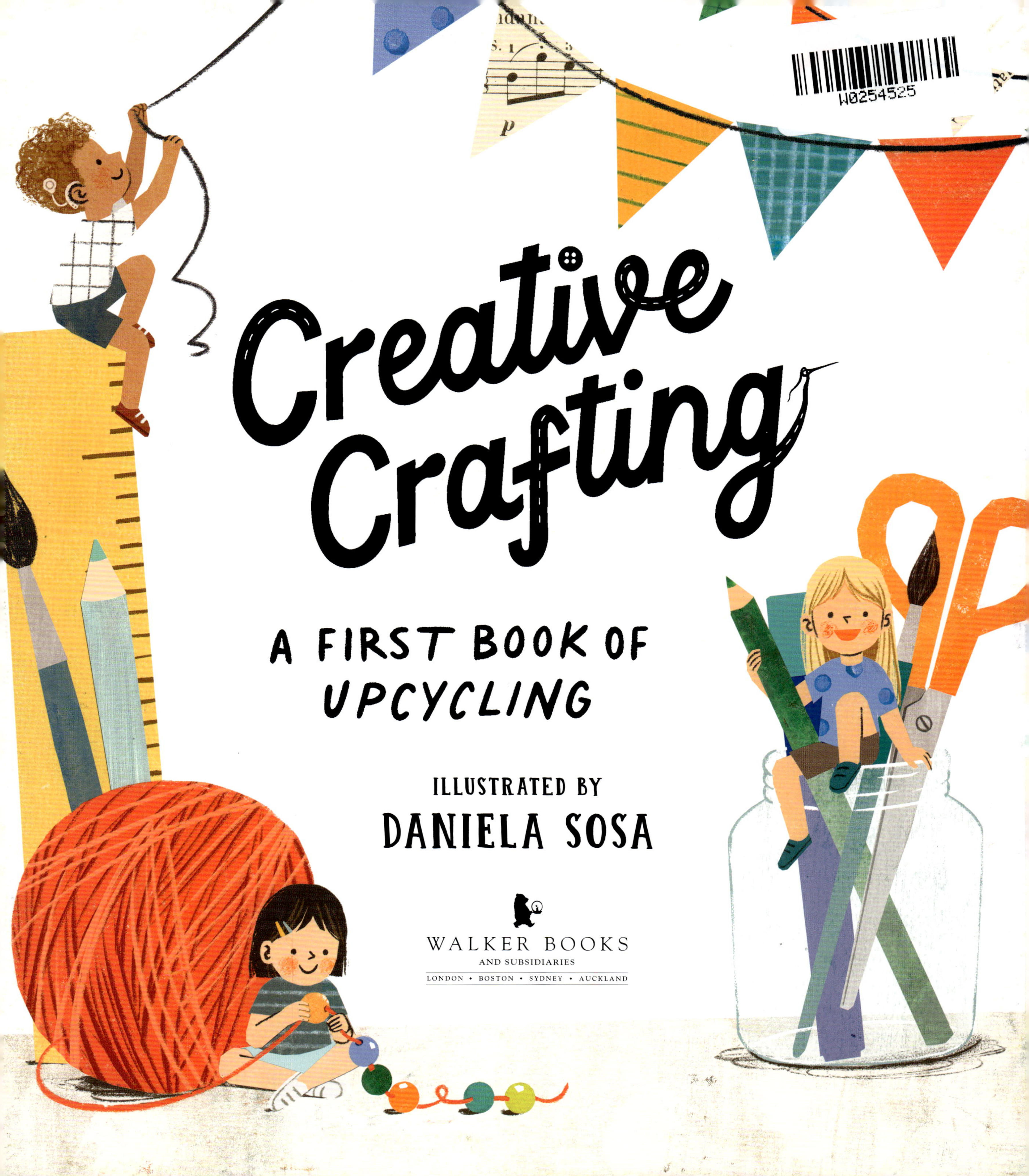

Creative Crafting

A FIRST BOOK OF UPCYCLING

ILLUSTRATED BY
DANIELA SOSA

WALKER BOOKS
AND SUBSIDIARIES
LONDON • BOSTON • SYDNEY • AUCKLAND

CONTENTS

GETTING STARTED

Upcycling means making something new out of something else, and it's a brilliant way of being kind to the planet.

We all know that we need to recycle, but finding a new use for things that would have otherwise been thrown away keeps them out of landfill. And what you make could be even more useful – and lovely – than it was originally. With a little bit of imagination and creative know-how, you can take old bits and bobs from your rubbish and give them a new lease of life: as something practical or decorative for yourself, your friends or your family.

Why not start an upcycling box to store things you could use for projects? Create a stash of things to use again: toilet-roll tubes, yoghurt pots, old gift wrap, plastic drinks bottles, magazines, jars, tins, fruit punnets, sweet wrappers ... anything! When you wear out the knees on a pair of jeans, don't throw them away – you never know when they might come in handy. Even old T-shirts can be useful, for all kinds of things.

So what are you waiting for? Let's get crafting! Turn your trash into treasure, learn some new skills and have fun making something totally unique!

SPARE SOCK JUGGLING BALLS

YOU WILL NEED:

- Three socks
- Three handfuls of uncooked rice or lentils

Have you ever wanted to learn to juggle? This is your chance! Make your own juggling balls, then see if you can find an online tutorial to help you learn a new skill. This is also an excellent way to use up odd socks!

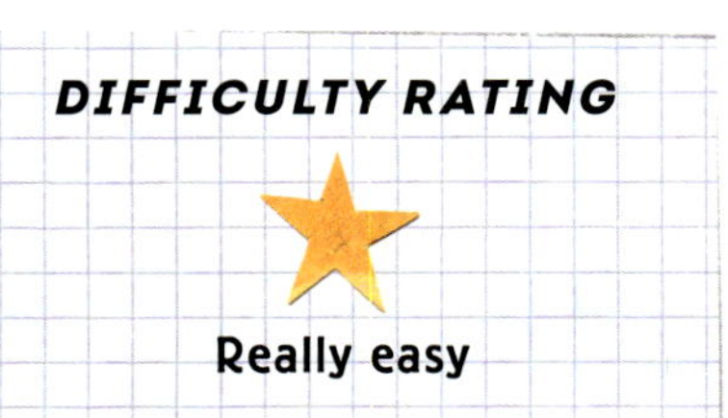

HOW TO MAKE:

1 Grab a handful of uncooked rice or lentils and drop it into the bottom of one of your socks.

2 Twist the open end of the sock tightly, as close to the rice or lentils as you can.

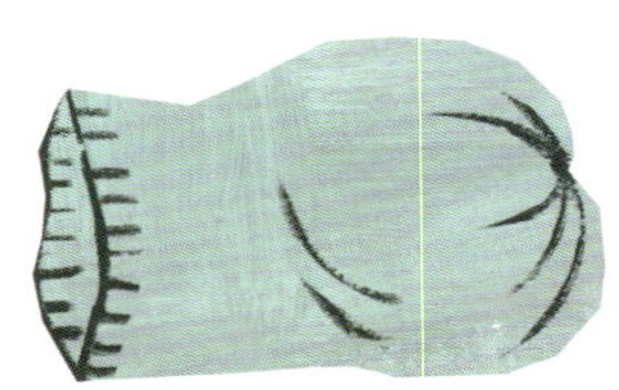

3 Fold the open end of the sock back over itself so that the opening is on the opposite side.

4 Twist it tightly again and turn it back on itself. You should now have a juggling ball.

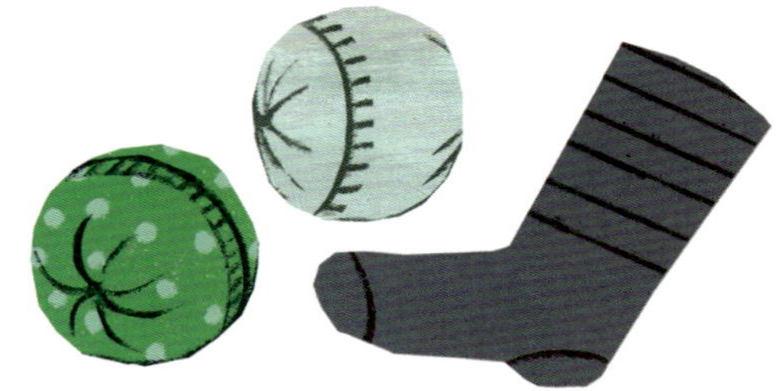

5 Repeat twice more with the other two socks, making sure that they are roughly the same weight.

BEDROOM BUNTING

This is a really quick and easy way to brighten up any dark corners in your bedroom.

HOW TO MAKE:

1 Cut your paper into long triangles. They don't have to be perfect but try and make them the same size.

2 When you have about 20 triangles, use a hole punch to make holes in the two corners at each end of the short side of your triangle.

3 Thread your ribbon or string through the holes.

4 Space out the triangles so that they are a few centimetres apart.

5 Ask a grown-up to help you hang up the finished bunting in your bedroom.

YOU WILL NEED:

- Colourful paper – old gift wrap or pages from comics work really well
- Scissors
- A hole punch
- A length of ribbon or string

TOP TIP!

If you are using a page from your favourite comic, you can cut it in half lengthways, then cut diagonal lines along it, to make lots of triangles really quickly.

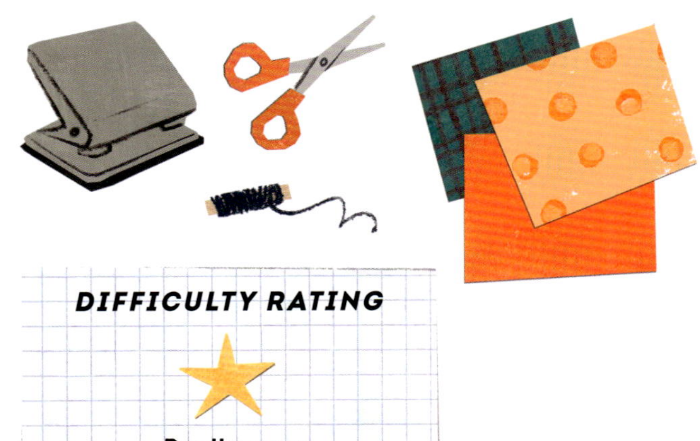

DIFFICULTY RATING

★

Really easy

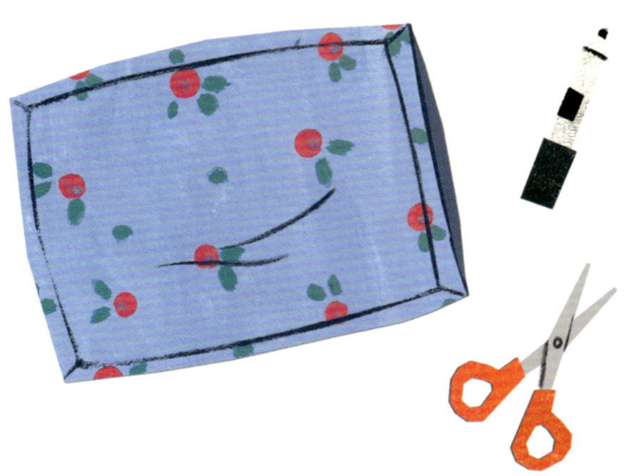

PILLOWCASE SHOPPING BAG

We are all trying to use less plastic, and remembering to take your own bag when you go shopping makes a big difference. You might find that there is an old pillowcase at home that you can use (make sure that you ask a grown-up first), but if not, you can find them in most charity shops.

YOU WILL NEED:

- An old pillowcase
- A felt-tip pen
- Scissors

DIFFICULTY RATING

★

Really easy

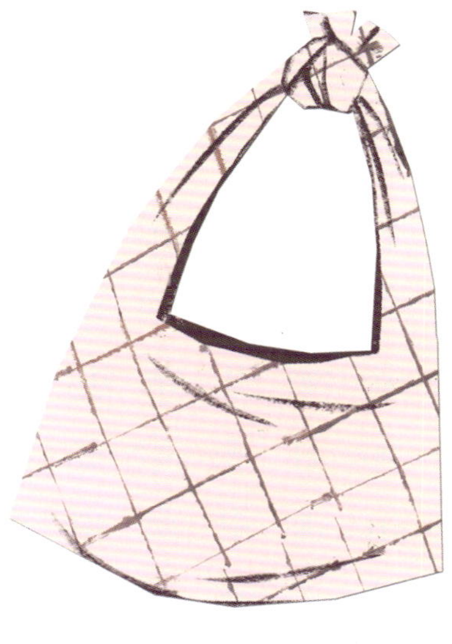

HOW TO MAKE:

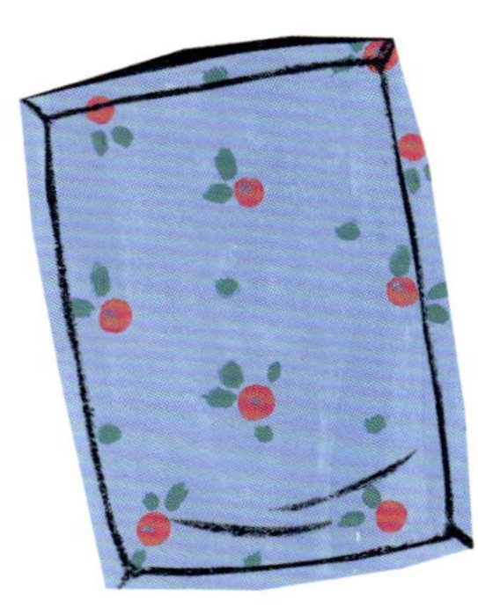

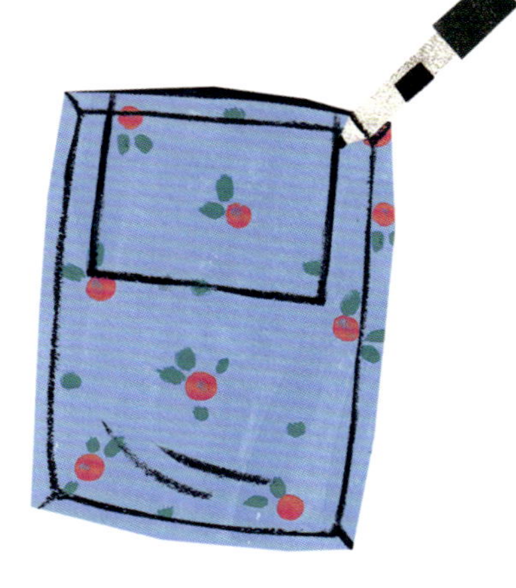

1. Lay your pillowcase out on a flat surface with the open end facing away from you.

2. Get your felt-tip pen and draw a big L on the left-hand side, starting at the open end and finishing halfway down.

3. Mirror this on the opposite side. (You should be able to see the bag taking shape.)

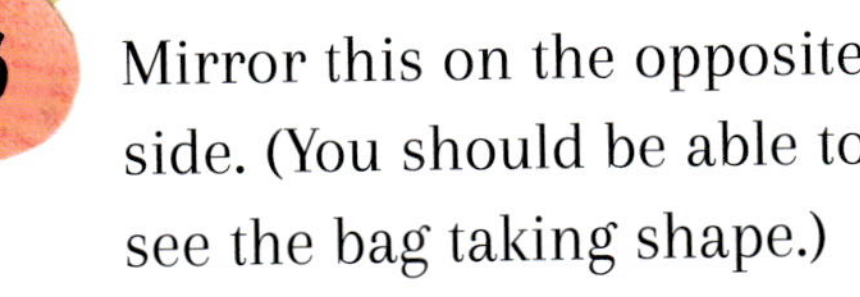
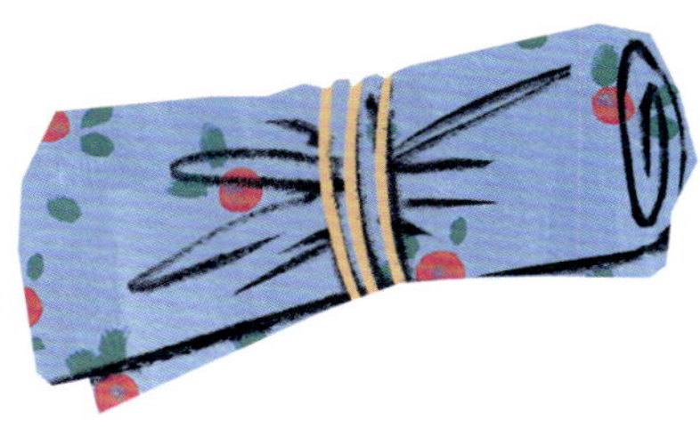

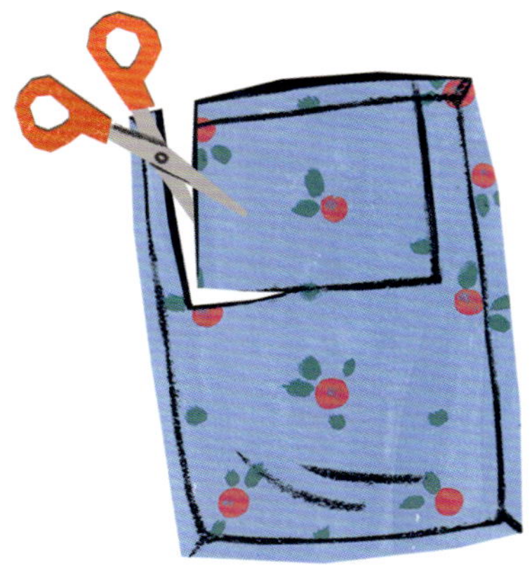

4. Using scissors, cut along the lines.

5. Tie the two sides of your bag's strap together in a really strong knot.

6. Roll it up, secure with an elastic band and keep it handy for the next time you go shopping.

DOUBLE-SIDED DOOR SIGN

Sometimes we all need a bit of peace and quiet, and this sign is the perfect way of letting your family know that you need a bit of alone time. Or to welcome them in! Choose your own words – it's up to you...

YOU WILL NEED:

- An old cereal box
- Scissors
- Glue
- Paints and a paintbrush
- Colouring pencils

DIFFICULTY RATING

Really easy

HOW TO MAKE:

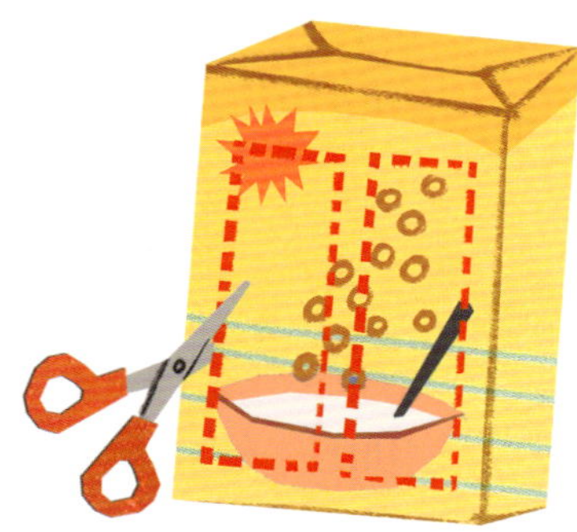

1. Using an old cereal box, cut out two rectangles 25 cm x 10 cm.
2. Stick them together with the coloured sides on the inside – this will make it easier to decorate later.
3. Leave a gap of about 3 cm from the top, then draw a circle with a diameter of approximately 6 cm.

TOP TIP!

Draw around the bottom of a small cup to get a really neat circle.

4 Draw a line from the right-hand edge to the right-hand side of your circle.

5 Cut along that line and then cut out the circle so that you end up with something that looks like this.

6 Use paints and pencils to decorate the hanger. Then write a message on each side of your door hanger.

GLITTER GLOBE

A calm jar is a lovely thing to have in your room. When you need a bit of quiet time, just give it a shake and watch it slowly settle. We've used glitter in ours – it has a lovely twinkly effect – but you can put in whatever you like as long as it's small and light. Even teeny, tiny toys can work well.

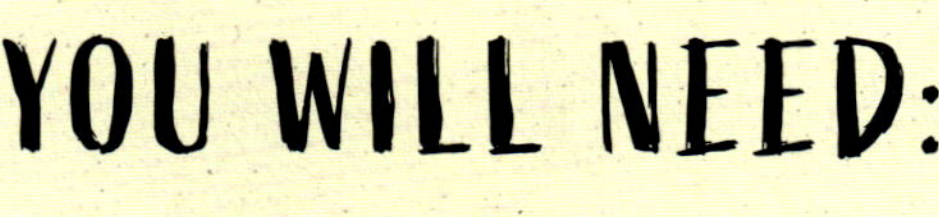

YOU WILL NEED:

- A jam jar or clear plastic bottle
- Water
- Glycerin (you can buy this from chemists and health food shops)
- Washing-up liquid
- Biodegradable glitter
- Old beads or sequins

HOW TO MAKE:

1 Remove any labels and wash out your jar (or bottle) really well.

2 Fill two thirds of the jar with water and then pour in the glycerin until the jar (or bottle) is nearly full.

3 Add two or three drops of washing-up liquid.

4 Drop in your chosen decorations.

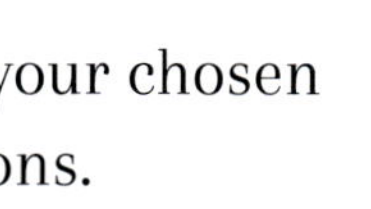

5 Screw the lid back on really tightly.

6 Shake and watch!

DIFFICULTY RATING

★

Really easy

DENIM POCKET PURSE

This makes a lovely shoulder bag that you can keep for yourself or give as a present to a friend. To make a bigger bag, you can use an adult-sized pair of jeans. Always keep old jeans that you've outgrown, or worn through at the knees – there are so many things you can make out of them!

YOU WILL NEED:

- An old pair of jeans
- Scissors
- Safety pins
- A needle and thread
- Badges, buttons, ribbon or anything else you want to use as decorations

HOW TO MAKE:

1 Carefully cut around the outside of one of the back pockets. You'll need to use quite sharp scissors, so ask a grown-up for help, if you need it.

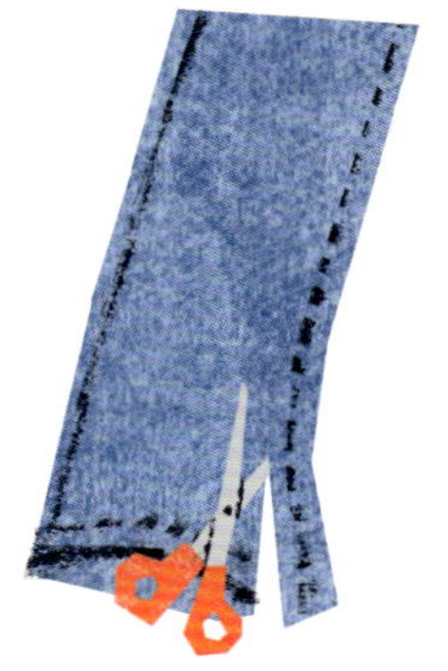

2 Make a long, thin strip by cutting down the outside seam on one of the legs. This is your strap. You could also use a length of ribbon if you'd prefer.

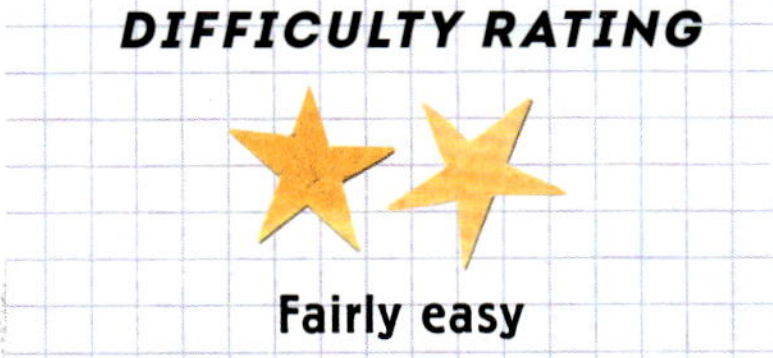

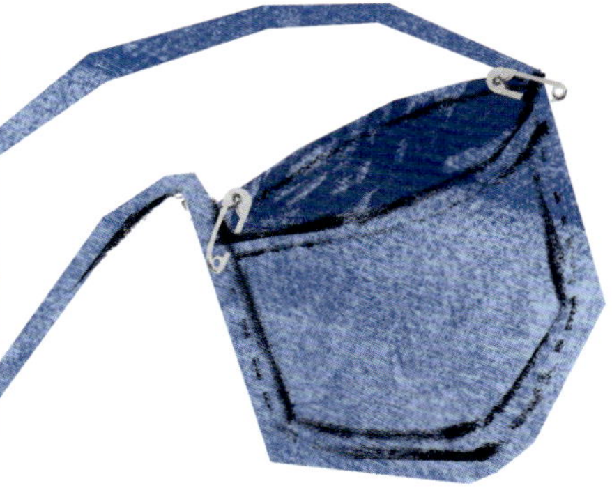

3 Ask your grown-up to pin the ends of the strap into the inside of the pocket, using safety pins.

4 Carefully sew the two ends in position.

5 Decorate the bag with badges or by sewing on buttons and ribbons.

TOILET-ROLL CAR GARAGE

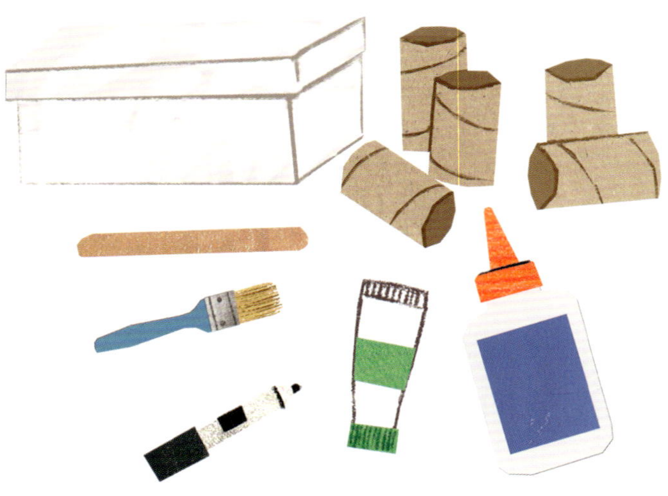

If your grown-ups are always telling you to tidy away your toy cars, this is the perfect project for you! You'll need quite a few toilet-roll tubes, so start saving them up until you have enough.

YOU WILL NEED:

- A shoe box
- Glue and a spreader
- Lots of toilet-roll tubes
- Paint and a paintbrush
- A felt-tip pen

HOW TO MAKE:

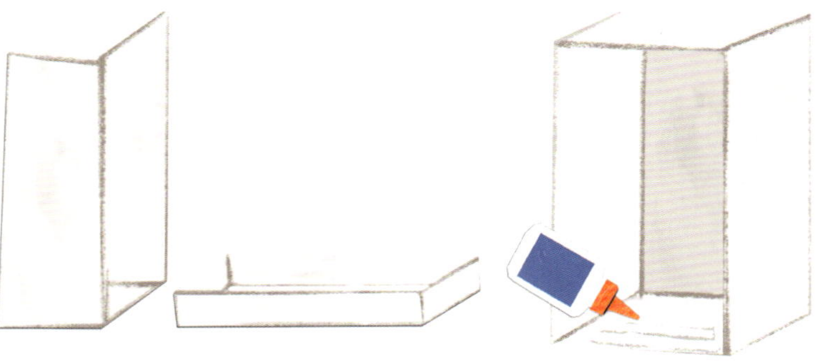

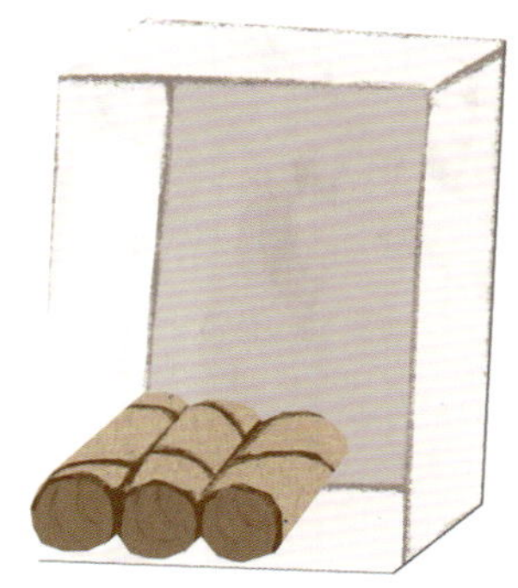

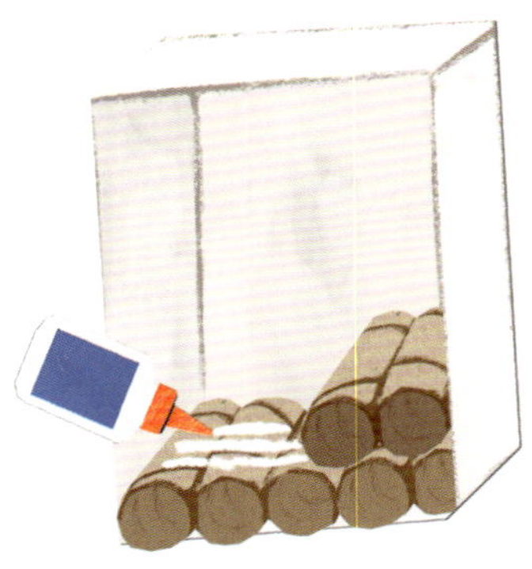

1. Take the lid off your shoe box and turn the box on its side, so that it is tall and thin.
2. Cover the inside bottom of the box with a layer of glue.
3. Start filling it with toilet-roll tubes, fitting in as many as you can.
4. Spread more glue along the top of your first layer and add another layer. They should fit together a bit like honeycomb.

TOP TIP!

You can use the same idea to make a hotel for animal figures or small dolls.

5. Keep going until you've completely filled the inside of the box.

6. Use the lid of your shoe box (upside down so that it doesn't hang over the top layer of parking) to make a sign for your garage.

7. Glue the lid in place and when the glue has dried, paint the top and sides of your garage.

8. Park your cars!

WOVEN PEN POT

Sometimes, a single-use cup is unavoidable, but when you've finished with it, don't throw it away, whatever you do! Keep it and turn it into something useful with this easy DIY.

YOU WILL NEED:

- A plastic or paper cup
- A tape measure
- A felt-tip pen
- Scissors
- A ball of wool
- Sticky tape

TOP TIP!
If you use thicker wool, the weaving will be quicker!

DIFFICULTY RATING
★★
Fairly easy

HOW TO MAKE:

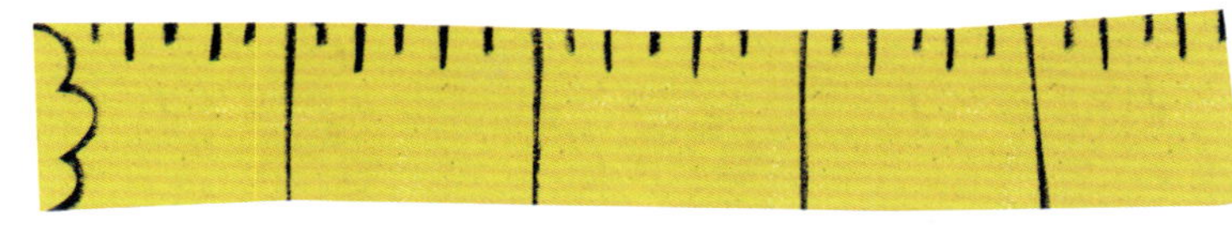

1 You need to make sure that you have an odd number of vertical "legs" to weave around, so first of all you need to measure the top edge of your cup.

2 Divide your measurement by seven and that will tell you how far apart you will need to space your legs. (For example, if your cup is 25 cm around, when you divide that by seven the top of each of your legs will be approximately 3.5 cm wide.)

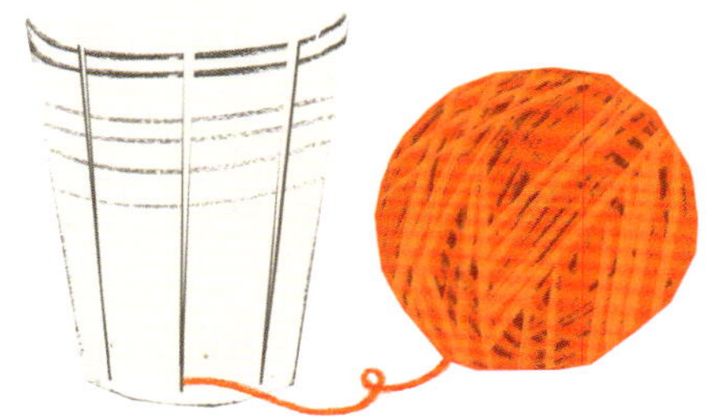

3 Mark out where you are going to start each of your legs.

4 Cut a straight line from each mark to the base of the cup. The legs will get narrower towards the bottom – that's OK!

5 Tie a knot in the end of your wool and slide it to the bottom of one of your cuts.

6 Begin weaving in and out of the legs, pushing the wool down as you go. Don't pull too tightly or the cup might lose its shape.

7 Swap colours if you run low, or fancy a change. Just tie the ends together in a knot and keep going.

8 When you get to the top, snip your wool and tape it neatly to the inside of your cup.

RAINBOW CRAYONS

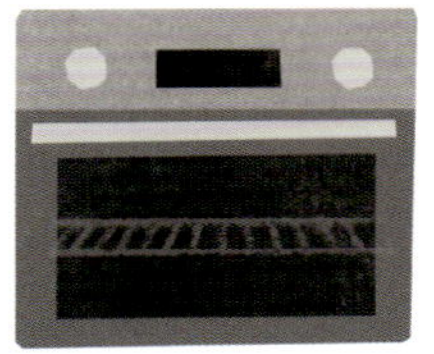

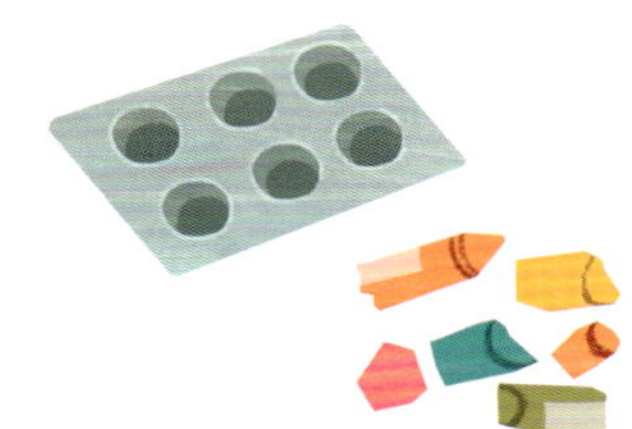

When your wax crayons get snapped or too worn down to use, it can be tempting to just throw them away. Keep the bits safe and you can give them a second lease of life with this clever hack!

YOU WILL NEED:

- Old pieces of wax crayon
- Silicone baking moulds
- A grown-up with oven gloves
- An oven

DIFFICULTY RATING

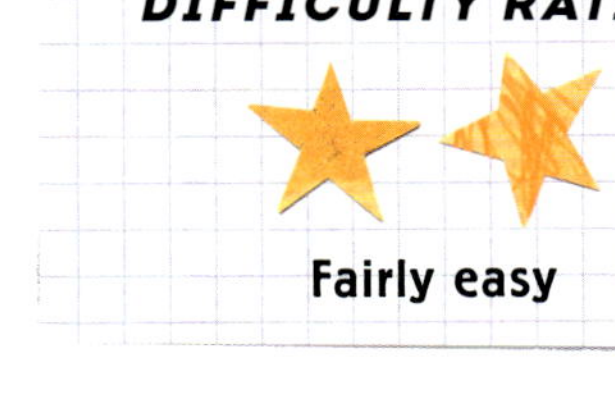

Fairly easy

HOW TO MAKE:

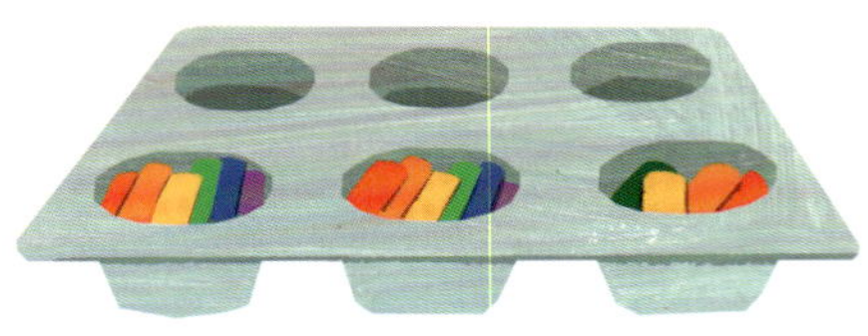

1 Make sure that you have taken all of the paper wrappers off your crayons. It can be a bit fiddly, but it's completely worth it.

2 Sort all of the pieces by colour and put them in rainbow order.

3 Pop the bits into the bottoms of the moulds, lining them up in colour order.

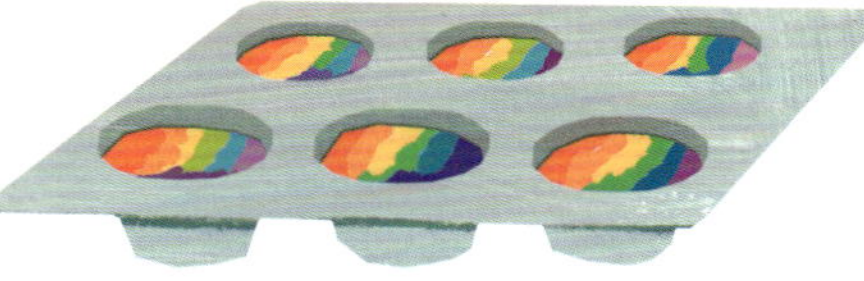

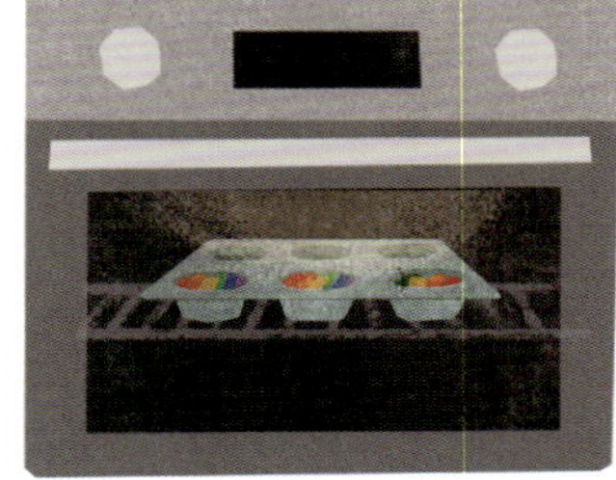

4 Pre-heat your oven to 180°C and ask your grown-up to put the moulds carefully onto one of the shelves.

5 Keep an eye on the crayons and ask your grown-up to take them out when they're completely melted. It should take about 15–20 minutes.

6 Let them cool completely, then pop them out and have fun creating rainbow drawings!

ANIMAL PLANTER

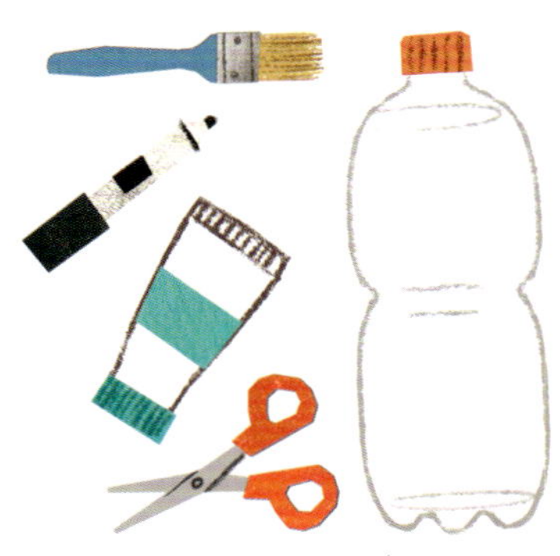

When you've finished with a 2-litre plastic drinks bottle, you can give it a new purpose by turning it into a super-cute animal plant pot holder.

TOP TIP!

Remember to choose a pot plant that's the right size to go inside your planter!

YOU WILL NEED:

- An empty 2-litre plastic bottle
- A permanent marker pen
- Scissors
- Acrylic paints and a paintbrush

DIFFICULTY RATING

★★★

Moderate

HOW TO MAKE:

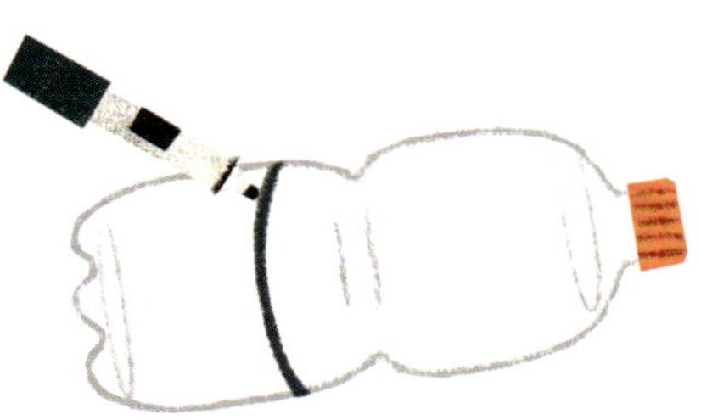

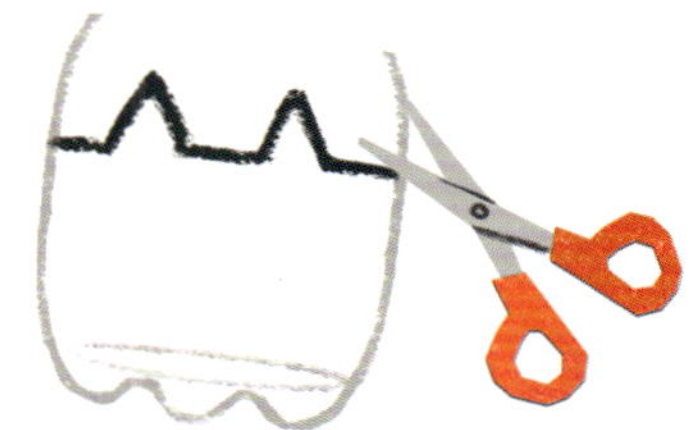

1. Draw a line about a third of the way up from the bottom.
2. Add a cute pair of ears to represent the animal you've chosen.
3. Cut along the line so that you have your basic pot holder. You'll probably need a grown-up to start you off.

4. Paint the outside of the pot holder with acrylic paint.
5. Bring your animal to life by drawing on eyes, a nose and whiskers.

COMIC BEAD NECKLACE

Raid your recycling for old comics or magazines to make this colourful necklace. The bright pages of comics make really fun beads, but you could just as easily use newspaper or left-over wrapping paper.

YOU WILL NEED:

- Paper
- Scissors
- A drinking straw or skewer
- Glue and a spreader
- String or ribbon

TOP TIP!

If you want a really chunky bead, make your first strip straight and then wind a second, triangular strip around the first one.

HOW TO MAKE:

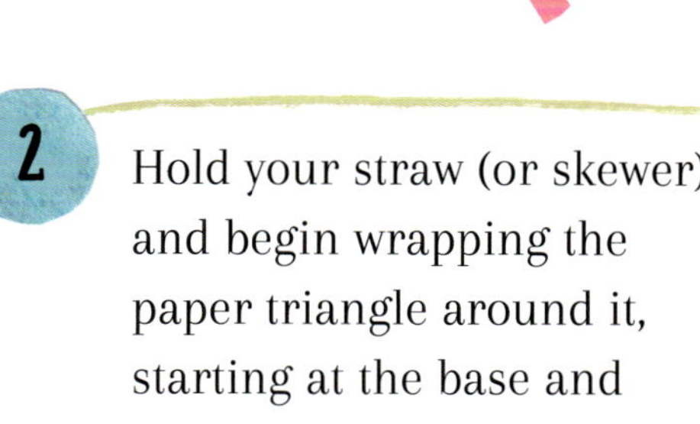

1 Cut your paper into long, thin triangular strips. The width at the base of your triangle will be how long your bead is, and the length of your triangle will affect how thick your bead is.

2 Hold your straw (or skewer) and begin wrapping the paper triangle around it, starting at the base and working towards the tip.

3 Roll it up as tightly as you can manage. This can be a bit tricky to start with but it gets easier the more you do.

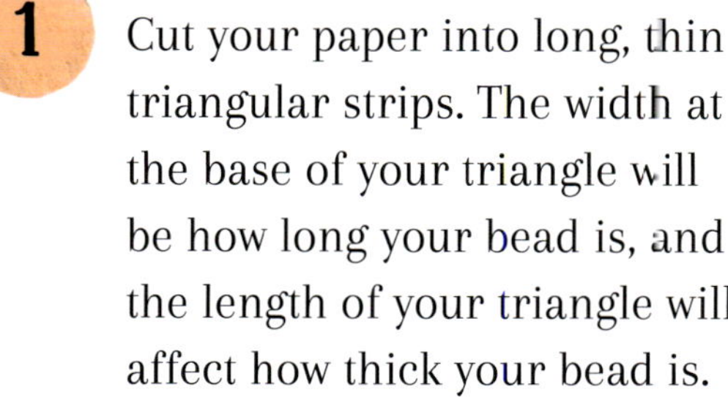

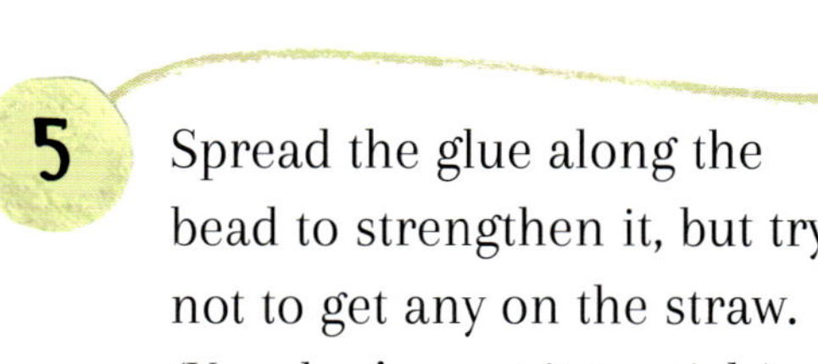

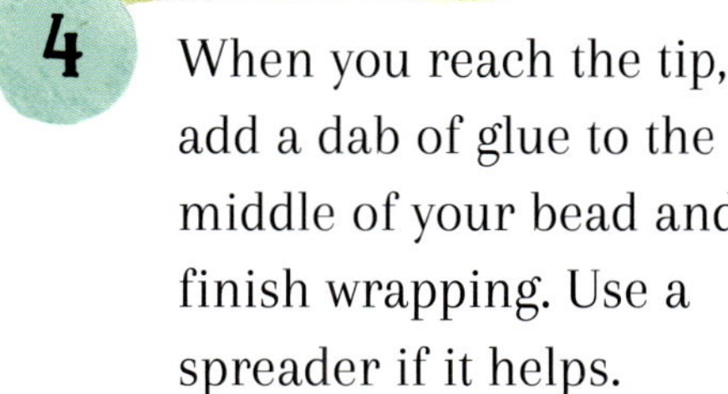

4 When you reach the tip, add a dab of glue to the middle of your bead and finish wrapping. Use a spreader if it helps.

5 Spread the glue along the bead to strengthen it, but try not to get any on the straw. (You don't want it to stick.)

6 Leave it to dry. You can work in batches and make a few beads on each straw.

7 When the beads are dry, slide them off and thread them onto a length of string or ribbon.

8 When you have enough beads, tie the ends of the string together, making sure that it's big enough to get it on and off over your head.

DENIM DOG TOY

An old pair of jeans makes a really strong toy for a dog to play with. Tie the knots as tightly as you can so that it will last as long as possible. If you made the denim pocket purse on page 13, you can use the legs for this project! Adult-sized jeans will make a bigger toy.

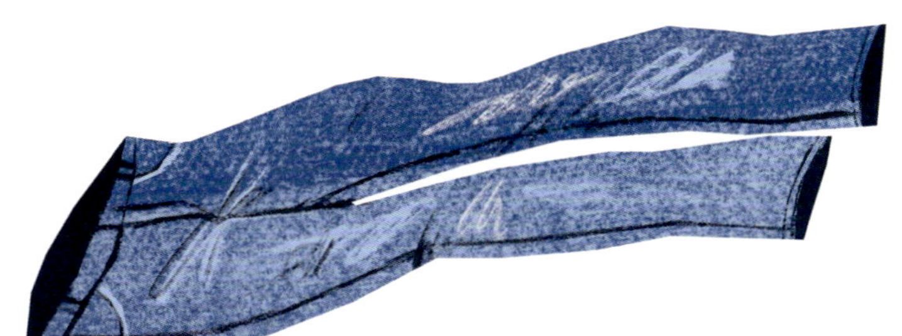

YOU WILL NEED:

- An old pair of jeans
- Scissors

HOW TO MAKE:

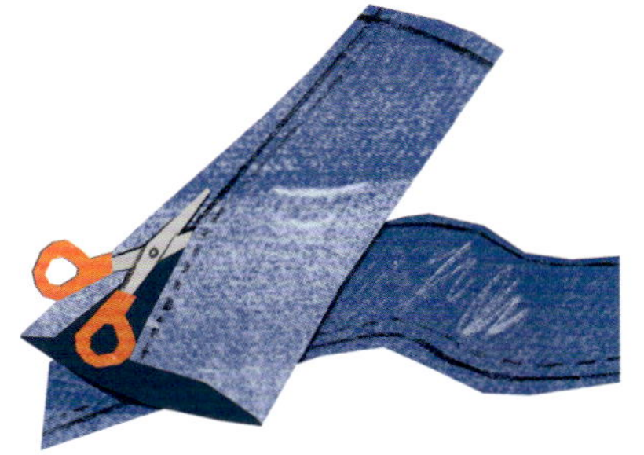

1. Cut both legs off an old pair of jeans.
2. Cut along the side seams and open them out.
3. Cut four long strips about 10 cm wide.
4. Tie them together in a knot as near one end of the strips as you can.

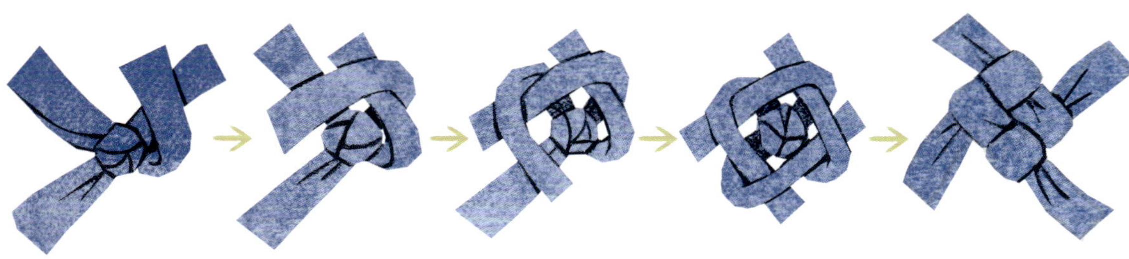

5. With the knot underneath, spread out the "legs" of your toy at right angles.
6. Follow the steps in the pictures above to create a column of box knots. These can be a bit fiddly, but once you get the hang of them, it gets a lot easier.

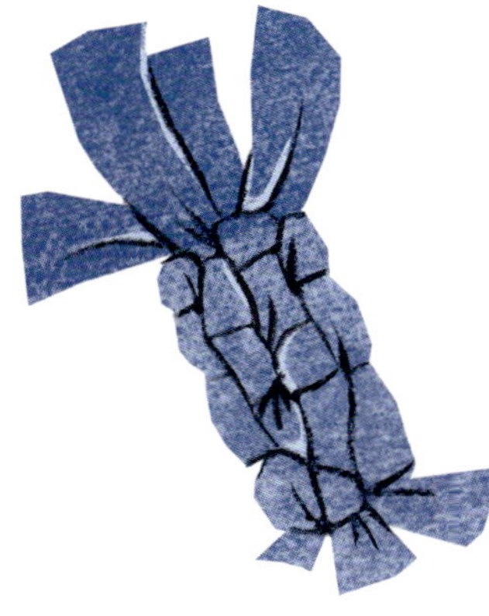
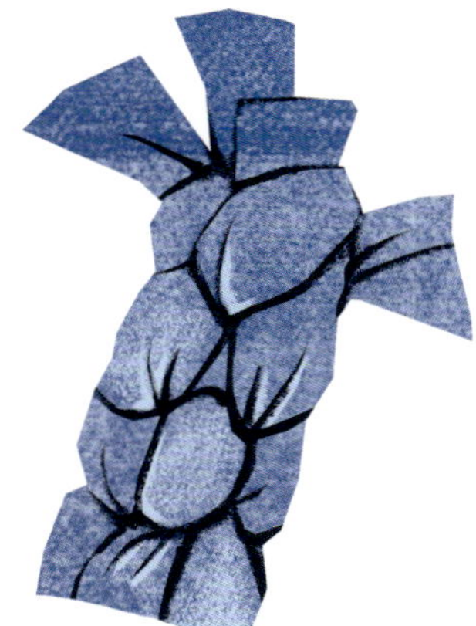
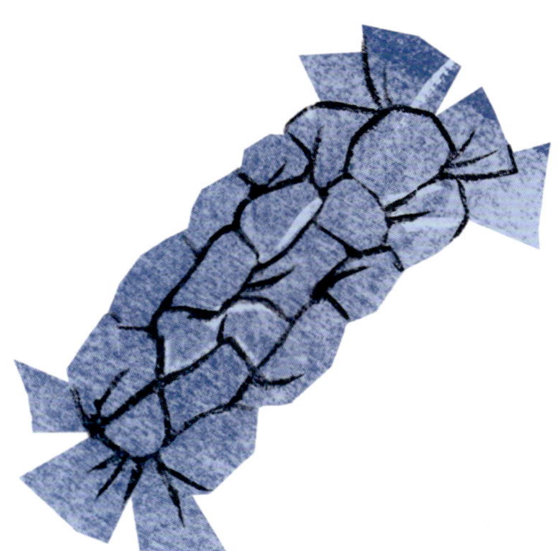

7. Pull it tight between each knot and repeat these steps until you have about 10 cm left.
8. Tie all four legs in a really firm knot.

DREAM-CATCHER

This decorative craft will make a beautiful addition to your bedroom. You can be as creative as you like – make it your own.

YOU WILL NEED:

- A large piece of cardboard (a box from your recycling is perfect)
- A pencil
- A dinner plate
- Scissors
- A hole punch
- Sticky tape
- Coloured wools and ribbons
- A darning needle
- Beads and other decorative items
- Scraps of fabric

HOW TO MAKE:

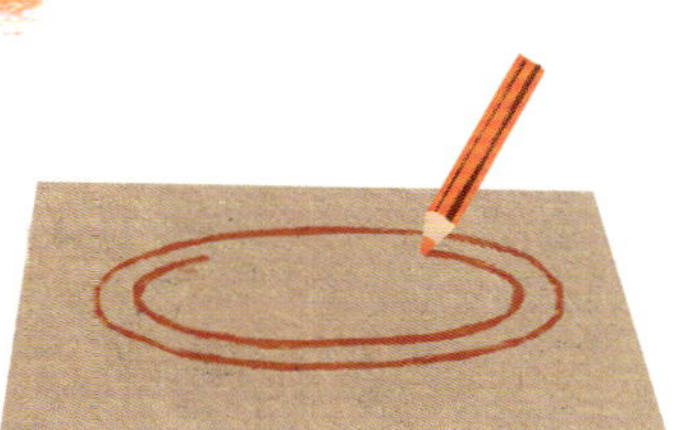

1. Lay your piece of card-board on the floor and, using a dinner plate, draw a large circle.

2. Draw a second line about 2 cm inside your circle.

3. Cut along the outside line and then cut out the inner circle so that you're left with a ring. You might need to ask a grown-up to help.

4. Use the punch to make holes in the ring, about 3 cm apart.

5. Tie a knot in one end of a length of wool or ribbon and secure it to the back of the ring with sticky tape. Thread the other end onto your darning needle and start to thread it across the centre from one hole to another.

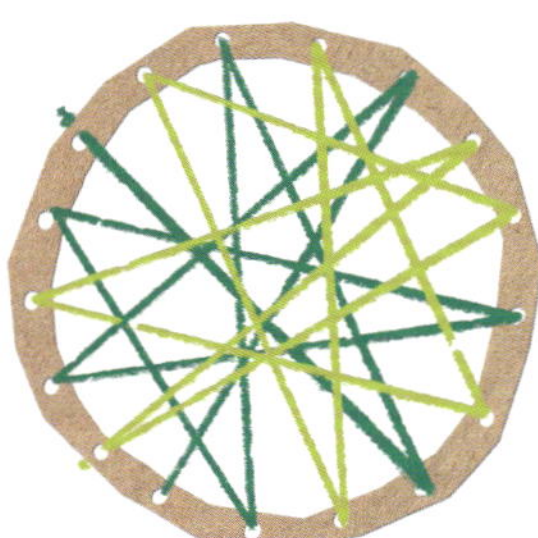

6. It doesn't need to look neat or symmetrical, and you can use as many different strands as you like. When it's finished, tie off your end.

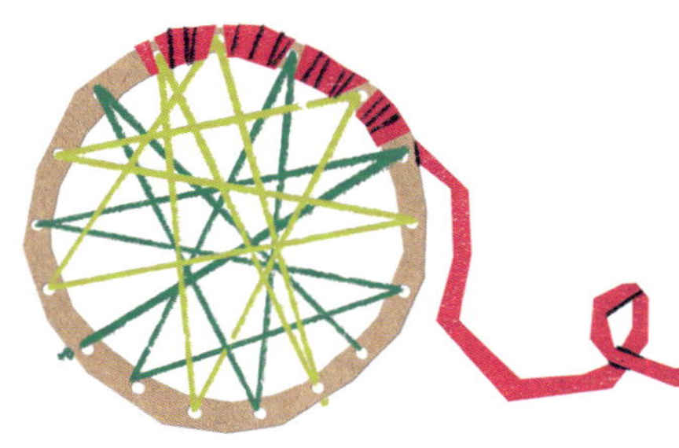

7. Wrap a new piece of ribbon around your ring, weaving it in between the cross threads, until you can't see the cardboard.

8. Now it's time to decorate! Use more wool and ribbons and tie them to the bottom of your ring.

9. Thread beads onto some of them and secure them with knots. Cut feather shapes out of the scraps of fabric and tie them on as well.

10. When you're happy with your dreamcatcher, hang it up in your bedroom and enjoy sweet dreams!

TOILET-ROLL KALEIDOSCOPE

This is a lovely project that you can make from your recycling and give as a present to a friend.

YOU WILL NEED:

- A toilet-roll tube
- Paints and a paintbrush or coloured paper and glue
- A piece of cardboard (approximately 10 cm x 15 cm)
- Kitchen foil
- Sticky tape
- Clear plastic (a fruit punnet from your recycling is ideal)
- A felt-tip pen
- Scissors
- Sequins, beads, sweet wrappers and other little bits and bobs

TOP TIP!

Hold your kaleidoscope up to a light and turn it. You should see lots of amazing patterns!

HOW TO MAKE:

1 Start off by decorating the outside of your toilet-roll tube. You can use any colour paint you like, wrap it with colourful paper – or even cover it with stickers.

2 Fold the piece of cardboard widthways into thirds. Make sure that the prism slots inside the tube.

3 Unfold it and carefully glue a layer of kitchen foil on one side. Try and keep the foil as smooth as you can.

4 Fold the cardboard into a triangular prism with the foil on the inside and secure the edges with tape.

5 Place the end of the toilet-roll onto clear plastic and draw around it with a felt-tip pen. Repeat so that you have two circles.

6 Cut one out, placing your scissors just inside the line so that it is slightly smaller than the toilet-roll.

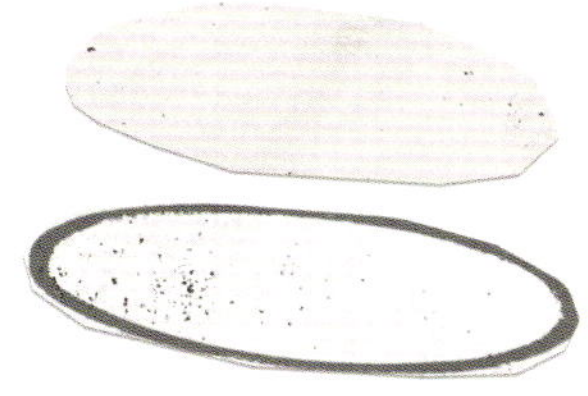

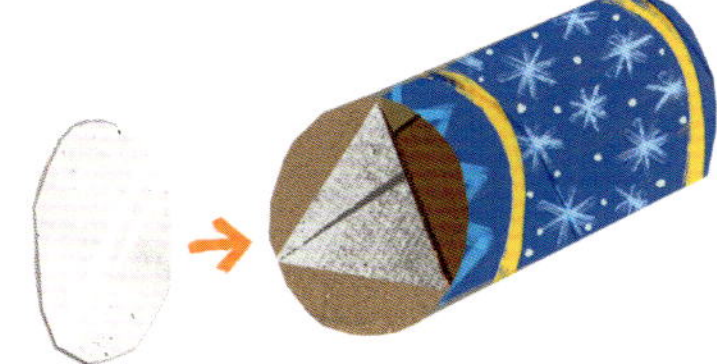

7 Cut out the second circle, this time placing your scissors just outside the line so that it is slightly larger than the toilet roll.

8 Slot the prism into the tube and drop the smaller disc onto one end. Secure with tape.

9 Sprinkle in beads, sequins and whatever other decorative elements you want in your kaleidoscope.

10 Place the larger plastic disc on the outside of the tube and tape over the edges so that your decorations are safely contained.

SEED-PAPER GIFT CARDS

These cards – made from your own recycled paper – double up as really special presents. When the person you have given them to has finished with them, they can take the seed-paper decorations off, plant them in some soil and grow their own flowers!

YOU WILL NEED:

- A covering to protect your work surface
- Scraps of old paper or envelopes (lighter colours work better for this project)
- A grown-up
- A blender
- Warm water
- Flower seeds (bee-friendly are best)
- A washing-up cloth or tea towel
- A large, flat dish
- An old sponge
- A5 sheets of card
- Glue

HOW TO MAKE:

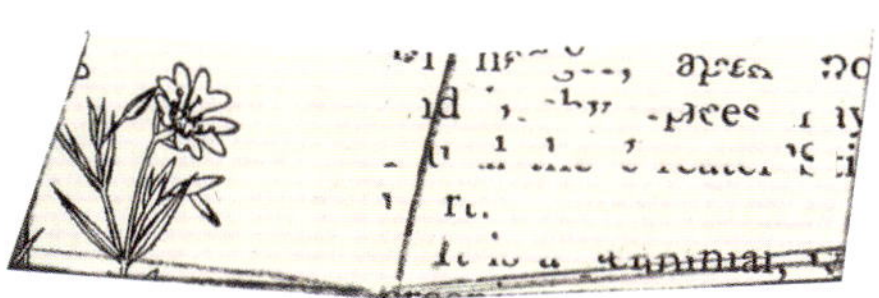

1 This one can get a bit messy, so make sure that you cover your work surface with old newspapers or a plastic tablecloth.

2 Gather together the scraps of paper that you are going to use. Your finished paper will be the same colour as your scraps.

3 Tear the paper into lots and lots of little pieces.

4 Ask your grown-up to half-fill the blender with warm water, then top up to the maximum fill line with your scraps.

5 Get your grown-up to pulse the mix, until you have as smooth a pulp as possible.

6 Stir in your flower seeds, but don't blend the mixture again.

7 Now prepare your dish by lining it with a washing-up cloth or tea towel.

8 Pour the mix on top of the cloth, making sure that the pulp is evenly spread out.

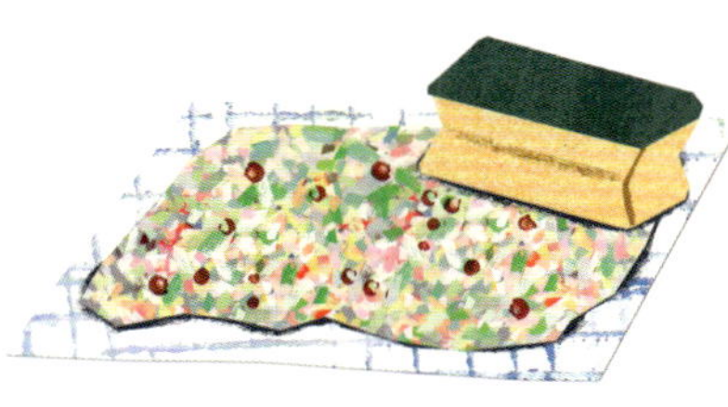

9 Slowly remove the cloth from the dish and carefully lay it somewhere flat. Press out any excess moisture with a sponge and leave to dry, patching up any holes.

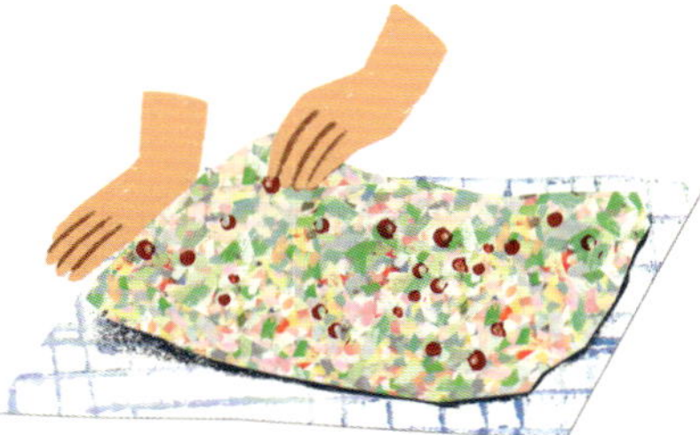

10 When it's completely dry, peel your seed-paper off the cloth.

11 When you're ready, fold your sheets of card in half, so that you have blank cards.

12 Cut shapes out of your seed-paper (flowers work well) and stick them to the fronts of your cards.

TIN-CAN TEALIGHT

Make a beautiful decoration for your garden in summer or for inside your house on long winter evenings. You'll need a grown-up to help you with this one.

YOU WILL NEED:

- An empty tin can, washed and with the label removed
- A permanent marker pen
- A grown-up
- A nail
- A hammer
- Acrylic paints and a paintbrush
- A battery-powered tealight

HOW TO MAKE:

1. Decide which shape you would like to have on your tealight holder. It could be a star, a heart – you choose! Draw it on the outside of the tin with a permanent marker pen.

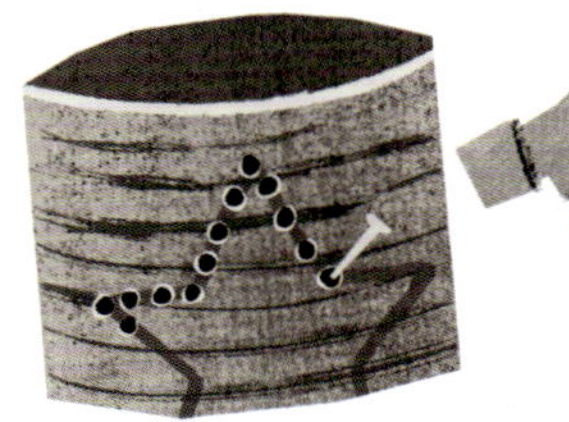

2. Ask your grown-up to use the hammer and nail to punch holes a few millimetres apart along the line of your shape.

3. Paint the outside of the tin using acrylic paints.

4. Pop a tealight in the can and watch it twinkle.

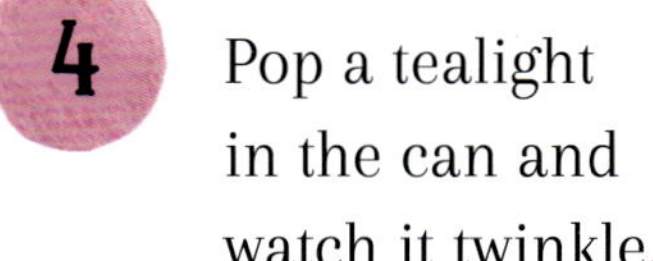

TOP TIP!

Filling the can with water and freezing it ahead of time means you can hammer in the nails without denting the metal. (You'll still need a grown-up to help, though.)